Commerce
&
Retail Management

:: Author ::

Pareshkumar M. Thakor

PUBLISHED BY

The New Era International Publishing House
HQ. At & Po. Chaveli., Ta- Chansma,
Dist- Patan, North Gujarat, India, Asia.
www.iphouseindia.com

First Publication: 14th April, 2015

ISBN:- 978-15-12121-88-9

Price: Rs.750/- INDIA

$ 15 OUTSIDE INDIA

PUBLISHED BY

The New Era International Publishing House
HQ. At & Po. Chaveli., Ta- Chansma,
Dist- Patan, North Gujarat, India, Asia.
www.iphouseindia.com

Understanding Retail - What is Retail ?

Before understanding the concept of retail, let us first go through few terminologies.

- **Market** - Any system or place where parties are engaged in exchange of either goods or services is called as market. The parties are often called as buyers and sellers. The seller offers his goods or services to the buyer who in return purchases it in exchange of money.
- **Goods** - Tangible (things which can be seen and touched) physical products which are transferred from a seller to the buyer (consumer) to fulfill the latter's need are called as goods.

Jack owned two laptops which he sold to Mike. In this case Jack is the seller while Mike is the buyer. Laptops are the goods which were earlier in Jack's custody and now belong to Mike.

What is Retail ?

Retail involves the sale of goods from a single point (malls, markets, department stores etc) directly to the consumer in small quantities for his end use. In a layman's language, retailing is nothing but transaction of goods between the seller and the end user as a single unit (piece) or in small quantities to satisfy the needs of the individual and for his direct consumption.

Let us understand the concept with the help of an example.

Tim wanted to purchase a mobile handset. He went to the nearby store and purchased one for himself.

In the above case, Tim is the buyer who went to a fixed location (in this case the nearby store). He purchased a mobile handset (Quantity - One) to be used by him. An example of retail.

The store from where Tim purchased the handset must have shown him several options for him to select one according to his budget and need.

From where do you think the store owner (also called the retailer) purchased all the handsets?

Here the manufacturers and the wholesalers come into the picture.

The retailers purchase goods in bulk quantities (huge numbers) to be sold to the end-users either directly from the manufacturers or through a wholesaler.

The Supply chain

Manufacturers.........................Retailers................End   User
                                                            (Consumer)

        Wholesalers

- **Manufacturers** - Manufacturers are the ones who are involved in production of goods with the help of machines, labour and raw materials.
- **Wholesaler** - The wholesaler is the one who purchases the goods from the manufacturers and sells to the retailers in large numbers but at a lower price. A wholesaler never sells goods directly to the end users.
- **Retailer** - A retailer comes at the end of the supply chain who sells the products in small quantities to the end users as per their requirement and need.

The end user goes to the retailer to buy the goods (products) in small quantities to satisfy his needs and demands. The complete process is also called as Shopping.

- **Shopping** - The process of purchasing products by the consumer is called as shopping. However there are certain cases where shopping does not always end in buying of products. Sometimes individuals do go for shopping but return home empty handed. Such a shopping is merely for fun and is called window shopping. In window shopping, individuals generally go to the market, check out various options and their prices but do not buy anything. This kind of shopping helps to break the monotony.

Types of Retail Outlets

Retailing refers to a process where the retailer sells the goods directly to the end-user for his own consumption in small quantities.

Types of Retail outlets

- ### Department Stores

  A department store is a set-up which offers wide range of products to the end-users under one roof. In a department store, the consumers can get almost all the products they aspire to shop at one place only. Department stores provide a wide range of options to the consumers and thus fulfill all their shopping needs.

  Merchandise:
  Electronic   Appliances
  Apparels
  Jewellery
  Toiletries
  Cosmetics
  Footwear
  Sportswear
  Toys
  Books
  CDs, DVDs

  Examples - Shoppers Stop, Pantaloon

- ## Discount Stores

Discount stores also offer a huge range of products to the end-users but at a discounted rate. The discount stores generally offer a limited range and the quality in certain cases might be a little inferior as compared to the department stores.

Wal-Mart currently operates more than 1300 discount stores in United States. In India Vishal Mega Mart comes under discount store.

Merchandise:
Almost same as department store but at a cheaper price.

- ## Supermarket

A retail store which generally sells food products and household items, properly placed and arranged in specific departments is called a supermarket. A supermarket is an advanced form of the small grocery stores and caters to the household needs of the consumer. The various food products (meat, vegetables, dairy products, juices etc) are all properly displayed at their respective departments to catch the attention of the customers and for them to pick any merchandise depending on their choice and need.

Merchandise:
Bakery   products
Cereals

Meat   Products,   Fish   products
Breads
Medicines
Vegetables
Fruits
Soft   drinks
Frozen   Food
Canned Juices

- ## Warehouse Stores

A retail format which sells limited stock in bulk at a discounted rate is called as warehouse store. Warehouse stores do not bother much about the interiors of the store and the products are not properly displayed.

- ## Mom and Pop Store (also called Kirana Store in India)

Mom and Pop stores are the small stores run by individuals in the nearby locality to cater to daily needs of the consumers staying in the vicinity. They offer selected items and are not at all organized. The size of the store would not be very big and depends on the land available to the owner. They wouldn't offer high-end products.

Merchandise:
Eggs
Bread
Stationery

Toys
Cigarettes
Cereals
Pulses
Medicines

- **Speciality Stores**

As the name suggests, Speciality store would specialize in a particular product and would not sell anything else apart from the specific range.Speciality stores sell only selective items of one particular brand to the consumers and primarily focus on high customer satisfaction.

Example -You will find only Reebok merchandise at Reebok store and nothing else, thus making it a speciality store. You can never find Adidas shoes at a Reebok outlet.

- **Malls**

Many retail stores operating at one place form a mall. A mall would consist of several retail outlets each selling their own merchandise but at a common platform.

- **E Tailers**

Now a days the customers have the option of shopping while sitting at their homes. They can place their order through internet, pay with the help of debit or credit cards and the products are delivered at their homes only.

However, there are chances that the products ordered might not reach in the same condition as they were ordered. This kind of shopping is convenient for those who have a hectic schedule and are reluctant to go to retail outlets. In this kind of shopping; the transportation charges are borne by the consumer itself.

Example - EBAY, Rediff Shopping, Amazon

- **Dollar Stores**

Dollar stores offer selected products at extremely low rates but here the prices are fixed.

Example - 99 Store would offer all its merchandise at Rs 99 only. No further bargaining is entertained. However the quality of the product is always in doubt at the discount stores.

Retail Mechanism - How does retail work ?

Retailing is defined as the process of selling merchandise to the consumers for their end use in small quantities. The retailer sells products to the end-users either in single units or in small quantities as per their need and capability.

Retailer...............................Consumer
(End -
User)

Retailing

How does retail work ?

Let us now understand the various ways a consumer can purchase goods from the retailer.

- ## Counter service

  As the name suggests, counter service refers to the process of procuring the merchandise from the counter. The buyer does not have an easy access to the merchandise of the store and he can't pick up things on his own. In such a mechanism the buyer has to walk up to the counter and ask for his requirements.

  Example

  ## Jewellery Store

  Can you go to a jewellery store and pick up things on your own ? No

  You need to ask the sales person to show you the sample designs for you to finalize something as per your taste and pocket.

  ## Chemist Shop

  Chemist shop does not allow the buyers to simply walk into the store and pick up medicines. One needs to walk up to the counter, show his prescription from the doctor to get the medicines from the retailer.

- ## Delivery Service

The mechanism of shipping goods to the customer's doorsteps is called as delivery service. The end-user does not have to walk up to the store to procure his merchandise; instead the goods are directly delivered to his house through various means of transportation. Delivery service is a boon for the individuals who have an extremely busy life style and do not have enough time to walk up to the store.

Online Shopping

Internet has helped end-users to shop from their homes only. Online shopping sites like Amazon, eBay etc provide a wide range of options to the consumers who can order the desired merchandise through internet. Once the payment is done through debit or credit cards, the goods are delivered at the address the customer requests for. The transportation charges however are borne by the consumer himself.

Order through telephone

Now a days several restaurants and eating joints provide an option of ordering food while sitting at home. The food outlets upload their complete menu in the website providing a wide range of options to the end-users. One can easily place his order over the phone and the food is delivered at his doorstep within no time.

Pizza Hut, Dominos (Promise to deliver hot and crisp pizza within 30 minutes of placing the order)

- **Door To Door Sales:** Door to door sales is a process where the sales person travels from one house to the other and prompts the customers to buy the product. He gives the demo of his product and strives hard to convince the individual to buy the merchandise.

  Examples

  Eureka Forbes operates on this mechanism where experienced sales professional visits the doorsteps of the potential customers, gives them presentations and influences them to purchase the product.

  Telephone companies also sometimes rely on this mechanism to sell their connections.

- **Self Service:** In self service the individuals have the liberty to pick up merchandise on their own and help themselves.
- **Second Hand Retail:** In second hand retail shops the retailer sells second hand goods to the end-users. Such shops generally run for charity where people donate their used merchandise to be resold to the poor and needy free of cost.

Retail Pricing - Different Types of Pricing Models

The sale of goods from fixed points (malls, department stores, supermarkets and so on) to the consumer in small quantities for his own consumption is called as retail. According to the concept of retailing, a retailer doesn't sell products in bulk; instead sells the merchandise in small units to the end-users.

Retail Pricing

Cost Plus Pricing Mechanism

Every organization runs to earn profits and so is the retail industry.

Cost plus pricing works on the following principle:

- Cost Price of the product + Profit (Decided by the retailer) = Final price of the merchandise.

According to cost plus pricing strategy the retailer adds some extra amount to the actual cost price of the product to earn his share of profits. The final price of the merchandise includes the profit as decided by the retailer.

Cost Plus Pricing

- Cost plus pricing strategy takes into account the profit of the retailer.
- Cost plus pricing is an easy way to calculate the price of the merchandise.

- The increase in the retailer price of the merchandise is directly proportional to the increase in the cost price.
- The customers however do not have a say in cost plus pricing.

Manufacturer Suggested Retail Price (Also called List Price or Recommended retail price)

According to manufacturer suggested retail pricing strategy the retailer sets the final price of the merchandise as suggested by the manufacturer.

MSRP

- The retailer sells his merchandise at a price suggested by the manufacturer.

Condition 1

- The retailer sells the product at the same price as suggested by the manufacturer.

Condition 2

- The retailer sells the merchandise at a price less than what was suggested by the manufacturer - Such a condition arises when the retailer offers "Sale" on his merchandise.

Condition 3

- Retailers initially quote an unreasonably high price and then reduce the price on the customer's request to make him realize that a favour has been done to him. A condition of Bargain - where the customer negotiates with the retailer to reduce the price of the merchandise.

Competitive Pricing

The cut throat competition in the current retail scenario has prompted the retailers to guarantee excellent customer service to the buyers for them to prefer them over their competitors.

- The price of the merchandise is more or less similar to the competitor's but the retailers add on certain attractive benefits for the customers. (Longer payment term, gifts etc.)
- The retailers ensure that the customers leave their store with a smile to have an edge over the competitors.
- He tries his level best to offer better services to the customers for a better business in future.

Pricing Below Competition

According to pricing below competition policy

- The price of the merchandise is kept lesser than what is being offered by the competitors.

Prestige Pricing (Pricing above competition)

According to prestige pricing mechanism, the price of the merchandise is set slightly above the competitors.

The retailer can charge higher price than the competitors only under the following circumstances:

Exclusive Brands at the store.
Brand image of the store
Prime location of the retail store
Excellent customer service
Merchandise not available at any other store
Latest Trends

Psychological Pricing

- Certain price of a product at which the consumer willingly purchases it is called psychological price.
- The consumer perceives such prices to be correct.
- A retailer sets a psychological price which he feels would meet the expectations of the buyers and they would easily buy the merchandise.

Multiple Pricing

- According to multiple pricing, the retailer sells multiple products (more than one) for a single price.
- The retailers combine few products to be sold for a single fixed price.
- 3 Shirts for $100/- or 3 Perfumes for $20/- and so on.

Discount Pricing

According to discount pricing, the retailer sells his merchandise at a discounted price during off seasons or to clear out his stock.

Retail Merchandising

Merchandising

- Retail Merchandising refers to the various activities which contribute to the sale of products to the consumers for their end use. Every retail store has its own line of merchandise to offer to the customers. The display of the merchandise plays an important role in attracting the customers into the store and prompting them to purchase as well.
- Merchandising helps in the attractive display of the products at the store in order to increase their sale and generate revenues for the retail store.
- Merchandising helps in the sensible presentation of the products available for sale to entice the customers and make them a brand loyalist.

Promotional Merchandising

- The ways the products are displayed and stocked on the shelves play an important role in influencing the buying behavior of the individuals.

A merchandiser maximizes the sale of the products by:

Attractive packaging

The packaging of the merchandise goes a long way in improving the brand value of the product. A product kept in a nice box would definitely catch the attention of the customers.

Impressive presentation of the Product

The display of the products at the retail store must entice the customers. The merchandiser in coordination with the store manager must ensure that the products are according to the season as well as latest trends.

The merchandiser must:

- Source something which is unique and not available at any other retail store.
- Never compromise on quality of the merchandise. Compromising on quality costs later.
- Source merchandise as per the season and climate.

By mid of August and early September, the summer merchandise is generally on a close out and stores begin stocking merchandise for the winter season. Warm clothing, full sleeves apparels, jackets, pullovers start replacing cut sleeves, capris, ankle length dresses, shorts and so on. Colourful clothes dominate the shelves as compared to the subtle colours in summers.

The type of product sourced also depends on the climatic conditions of the place.

A Reebok store in Central India or Southern India would stock summer merchandise between April to September whereas a retail store under the same brand somewhere in a cold area would source woollen merchandise along with summer clothing as per the demand of the season.

Unique Pricing (Discounts)

Attractive prices, discounts, rebates also bring customers to the store.

Promotional schemes, gifts

Coupons and attractive gifts make shopping a pleasurable experience for the customers.

Merchandising Tips

- The merchandiser must source products according to the latest trends and season.
- The merchandise should be as per the age, sex and taste of the target market.
- Merchandise for children should be in line with cartoon characters (like Barbie, Pokemon etc) to excite them.

Creative Portico Pvt Ltd sources bed sheets, curtains specially inspired from characters (Disney, Harry Porter, Hannah Montana) - a hit amongst kids.

Youngsters prefer funky clothes (colourful T Shirts, faded denims) as compared to professionals who would go for subtle colours.

The target market of Zodiac Clothing Company Limited mainly comprises of office goers and professionals. The merchandise (shirts, trousers, neck ties, belts) is as per the taste of the professionals. Beach house shirts would have no takers in such a store.

- The merchandiser ideally works on the "invariant right" principle.

  Since most of us are right handed, it is a common tendency that customers entering into retail store would first go towards the right side of the store. The merchandiser should display the unique and expensive collections on the right side of the store to entice the customers.

- The set up of the store should be such that once a customer enters into a store, he has to walk through each and every department.
- The shelves should be stocked with the latest trends. The merchandise should be well organized on the racks according to their size and pattern.
- It is the key responsibility of the merchandiser to create an attractive display to pull the customers into the store. Once the customer steps into the store, he would definitely buy something or the other.

Cross Merchandising

Retailing refers to the concept of selling merchandise in small quantities to the consumers for their end use. According to retailing, the individual can walk up to any nearby retail store and purchase products as per his need and pocket in small units for his own consumption.

The display of merchandise at the store plays an important role in attracting the customers into the store. The display of the products at the retail store goes a long way in influencing the buying behaviour of the consumers. The presentation of the products is essential to create that first impression in the minds of the consumers.

Cross Merchandising

Cross merchandising refers to the display of opposite and unrelated products together to earn additional revenues for the store. Products from different categories are kept together at one place for the customers to find a relation among them and pick up all.

According to cross merchandising:

- Unrelated products are displayed together.
- The retailer makes profits by linking products which are not related in any sense and belong to different categories.

- Cross Merchandising helps the customers to know about the various options which would complement their product.
- Cross Merchandising makes shopping a pleasurable experience as it saves customer's precious time.

Examples of Cross Merchandising

- Mobile covers displayed next to mobile phones.
- Recharge coupons with new sim cards
- Batteries with electronic appliances
- Neck ties or cuff links displayed with men' shirt
- Fashion jewellery, rings, anklets, hand bags with female dresses
- Shoe laces, shoe shiners, shoe racks with shoes
- Audio CDs with CD Players

Jenny went to a nearby retail store to purchase a shirt for herself. She picked up a nice blue formal shirt displayed on the mannequin. The retailer was smart enough to add matching trouser, scarf and a handbag to the mannequin (Cross Merchandising). Not only did Jenny purchase the shirt but also the trouser as well as the office bag as she felt the products would complement her shirt.

The customer at the first instance can't really decide what all he needs apart from the products he has already purchased. **Through cross merchandising, the retailer smartly tries his level best to convince the customers to buy additional products apart from his existing list.**

Mike went to a nearby departmental store to purchase cigarettes. He spotted chewing gums displayed along with the cigarettes. He immediately decided to purchase the chewing gums along with his cigarettes which he might need after smoking. Thus cross merchandising (display of cigarettes along with chewing gum) made Mike realize the connection between the products and eventually pick both of them.

Important tips for Cross Merchandising

- The opposite products should be sensibly displayed for the customers to be able to relate them.
- The merchandise should be neatly arranged without giving a cluttered look to the store.
- The merchandise must complement each other to create the desired impact.
- **The retailer must make sure the products have some logical connection with each other**.

Displaying neck ties with Laptops would make no sense and fail to excite the customers. The customer would purchase either of the two (Either the Laptop or the neck tie) depending on his need but would never purchase both. However if laptop bags are kept with laptops, there are chances that the customer might pick up both the products.

- Use hangers, pegs, mannequins or suitable fixtures to intelligently display the unrelated goods and prompt the customer to pick all of them.

Visual Merchandising

The art of increasing the sale of products by effectively and sensibly displaying them at the retail outlet is called as visual merchandising. Visual merchandising refers to the aesthetic display of the merchandise to attract the potential buyers, prompt them to buy and eventually increase the sales of the store. In simpler words, visual merchandising is the art of displaying the merchandise to influence the consumer's buying behaviour.

The store must offer a positive ambience to the customers for them to enjoy their shopping.

The location of the products in the store has an important role in motivating the consumers to buy them. Sensible display of the merchandise goes a long way in influencing the buying decision of the individual.

The end-user will never notice something which is not well organized: instead stacked or thrown in heaps.

Proper Space, lighting, placing of dummies, colour of the walls, type of furniture,music, fragrance of the store all help in increasing the sale of the products.

Lighting is one of the critical aspects of visual merchandising. Lighting increases the visibility of the merchandise kept in the store. The store should be adequately lit and well ventilated. Avoid harsh lighting as it blinds the customers who walk into the store.

The signage displaying the name of the store or other necessary information must be installed properly outside the store at a place easily viewable to the customers even from a distance.

The retailer must be extremely cautious about the colour of the paint he chooses for his store. The paint colour can actually set the mood of the customers. The wall colours must be well coordinated with the carpet, floor tiles or the furnitures kept at the store. Dark colours make the room feel small and congested as compared to light and subtle colours.

The store must always smell good. Foul smell irritates the consumers and he would walk out of the store in no time. Use room fresheners 'or aromatic sticks for a pleasant environment.

The merchandise must be properly placed in display racks or shelves according to size and gender. Put necessary labels (size labels) on the shelves as it help the customers to locate the products easily. Make sure the product do not falls off the shelves as it gives a messy look.

The dummies should be intelligently placed and must highlight the unique collections, latest trends and new arrivals in order to catch the attention of the individual. The dummies should not act as an obstacle and should never be kept at the entrance of the store.

Don't play blaring music at the store. It acts as a hindrance to effective communication and the retailer can never understand what the buyer actually intends to buy.

Select the theme of the store according to the season. Red should be the dominating colour during Christmas or Valentines Day as the colour symbolizes love, fun and frolic. A white theme would look out of place during the season of love.

Don't keep unnecessary furniture as it gives a cluttered look to the store.

Why Visual Merchandising?

- Visual Merchandising helps the customers to easily find out what they are looking for.
- It helps the customers to know about the latest trends in fashion.
- The customer without any help can actually decide what he intends to buy.
- It increases the sales of the store and results in increased level of customer satisfaction.
- The customers can quickly decide what all they need and thus **visual merchandising makes shopping a pleasant experience**.

- Visual merchandising gives the store its unique image and makes it distinct from others.

Retail Management - Meaning and its Need

What is management ?

Management refers to the process of bringing people together on a common platform and make them work as a single unit to achieve the goals and objectives of an organization. Management is required in all aspects of life and forms an integral part of all businesses.

Retail management

The various processes which help the customers to procure the desired merchandise from the retail stores for their end use refer to retail management. Retail management includes all the steps required to bring the customers into the store and fulfill their buying needs.

Retail management makes shopping a pleasurable experience and ensures the customers leave the store with a smile. In simpler words, retail management helps customers shop without any difficulty.

Need for Retail Management - Why retail management ?

Peter wanted to gift his wife a nice watch on her birthday. He went to the nearby store to check out few options. The retailer took almost an hour to find the watches. This irritated

Peter and he vowed not to visit the store again.-An example of poor management.

You just can't afford to make the customer wait for long. The merchandise needs to be well organized to avoid unnecessary searching. Such situations are common in mom and pop stores (kirana stores). One can never enjoy shopping at such stores.

Retail management saves time and ensures the customers easily locate their desired merchandise and return home satisfied.

An effective management avoids unnecessary chaos at the store.

Effective Management controls shopliftings to a large extent.

- The retailer must keep a record of all the products coming into the store.
- The products must be well arranged on the assigned shelves according to size, colour, gender, patterns etc.
- Plan the store layout well.
- The range of products available at the store must be divided into small groups comprising of similar products. Such groups are called categories. A customer can simply walk up to a particular category and look for products without much assistance.
- A unique SKU code must be assigned to each and every product for easy tracking.

- Necessary labels must be put on the shelves for the customers to locate the merchandise on their own.
- Don't keep the customers waiting.
- Make sure the sales representatives attend the customers well. Assist them in their shopping. Greet them with a smile
- The retailer must ensure enough stock is available at the store.
- Make sure the store is kept clean. Don't stock unnecessary furniture as it gives a cluttered look to the store. The customers must be able to move freely.
- The store manager, department managers, cashier and all other employees should be trained from time to time to extract the best out of them. They should be well aware of their roles and responsibilities and customer oriented. They should be experts in their respective areas.
- The store manager must make daily sales reports to keep a track of the cash flow. Use softwares or maintain registers for the same.
- Remove the unsold merchandise from the shelves. Keep them somewhere else.
- Create an attractive display.
- Plan things well in advance to avoid confusions later on.
- Ask the customers to produce bills in case of exchange. Assign fixed timings for the same. Don't entertain customers after a week.

Retail Pricing - Different Types of Pricing Models

The sale of goods from fixed points (malls, department stores, supermarkets and so on) to the consumer in small quantities for his own consumption is called as retail. According to the concept of retailing, a retailer doesn't sell products in bulk; instead sells the merchandise in small units to the end-users.

Retail Pricing

Cost Plus Pricing Mechanism

Every organization runs to earn profits and so is the retail industry.

Cost plus pricing works on the following principle:

- Cost Price of the product + Profit (Decided by the retailer) = Final price of the merchandise.

According to cost plus pricing strategy the retailer adds some extra amount to the actual cost price of the product to earn his share of profits. The final price of the merchandise includes the profit as decided by the retailer.

Cost Plus Pricing

- Cost plus pricing strategy takes into account the profit of the retailer.
- Cost plus pricing is an easy way to calculate the price of the merchandise.

- The increase in the retailer price of the merchandise is directly proportional to the increase in the cost price.
- The customers however do not have a say in cost plus pricing.

Manufacturer Suggested Retail Price (Also called List Price or Recommended retail price)

According to manufacturer suggested retail pricing strategy the retailer sets the final price of the merchandise as suggested by the manufacturer.

MSRP

- The retailer sells his merchandise at a price suggested by the manufacturer.

Condition 1

- The retailer sells the product at the same price as suggested by the manufacturer.

Condition 2

- The retailer sells the merchandise at a price less than what was suggested by the manufacturer - Such a condition arises when the retailer offers "Sale" on his merchandise.

Condition 3

- Retailers initially quote an unreasonably high price and then reduce the price on the customer's request to make him realize that a favour has been done to him. A condition of Bargain - where the customer negotiates with the retailer to reduce the price of the merchandise.

Competitive Pricing

The cut throat competition in the current retail scenario has prompted the retailers to guarantee excellent customer service to the buyers for them to prefer them over their competitors.

- The price of the merchandise is more or less similar to the competitor's but the retailers add on certain attractive benefits for the customers. (Longer payment term, gifts etc.)
- The retailers ensure that the customers leave their store with a smile to have an edge over the competitors.
- He tries his level best to offer better services to the customers for a better business in future.

Pricing Below Competition

According to pricing below competition policy

- The price of the merchandise is kept lesser than what is being offered by the competitors.

Prestige Pricing (Pricing above competition)

According to prestige pricing mechanism, the price of the merchandise is set slightly above the competitors.

The retailer can charge higher price than the competitors only under the following circumstances:

Exclusive   Brands   at   the   store.
Brand   image   of   the   store
Prime   location   of   the   retail   store
Excellent   customer   service
Merchandise   not   available   at   any   other   store
Latest Trends

Psychological Pricing

- Certain price of a product at which the consumer willingly purchases it is called psychological price.
- The consumer perceives such prices to be correct.
- A retailer sets a psychological price which he feels would meet the expectations of the buyers and they would easily buy the merchandise.

Multiple Pricing

- According to multiple pricing, the retailer sells multiple products (more than one) for a single price.
- The retailers combine few products to be sold for a single fixed price.
- 3 Shirts for $100/- or 3 Perfumes for $20/- and so on.

Discount Pricing

According to discount pricing, the retailer sells his merchandise at a discounted price during off seasons or to clear out his stock.

Retail Merchandising

Merchandising

- Retail Merchandising refers to the various activities which contribute to the sale of products to the consumers for their end use. Every retail store has its own line of merchandise to offer to the customers. The display of the merchandise plays an important role in attracting the customers into the store and prompting them to purchase as well.
- Merchandising helps in the attractive display of the products at the store in order to increase their sale and generate revenues for the retail store.
- Merchandising helps in the sensible presentation of the products available for sale to entice the customers and make them a brand loyalist.

Promotional Merchandising

- The ways the products are displayed and stocked on the shelves play an important role in influencing the buying behavior of the individuals.

A merchandiser maximizes the sale of the products by:

Attractive packaging

The packaging of the merchandise goes a long way in improving the brand value of the product. A product kept in a nice box would definitely catch the attention of the customers.

Impressive presentation of the Product

The display of the products at the retail store must entice the customers. The merchandiser in coordination with the store manager must ensure that the products are according to the season as well as latest trends.

The merchandiser must:

- Source something which is unique and not available at any other retail store.
- Never compromise on quality of the merchandise. Compromising on quality costs later.
- Source merchandise as per the season and climate.

By mid of August and early September, the summer merchandise is generally on a close out and stores begin stocking merchandise for the winter season. Warm clothing, full sleeves apparels, jackets, pullovers start replacing cut sleeves, capris, ankle length dresses, shorts and so on. Colourful clothes dominate the shelves as compared to the subtle colours in summers.

The type of product sourced also depends on the climatic conditions of the place.

A Reebok store in Central India or Southern India would stock summer merchandise between April to September whereas a retail store under the same brand somewhere in a cold area would source woollen merchandise along with summer clothing as per the demand of the season.

Unique Pricing (Discounts)

Attractive prices, discounts, rebates also bring customers to the store.

Promotional schemes, gifts

Coupons and attractive gifts make shopping a pleasurable experience for the customers.

Merchandising Tips

- The merchandiser must source products according to the latest trends and season.
- The merchandise should be as per the age, sex and taste of the target market.
- Merchandise for children should be in line with cartoon characters (like Barbie, Pokemon etc) to excite them.

Creative Portico Pvt Ltd sources bed sheets, curtains specially inspired from characters (Disney, Harry Porter, Hannah Montana) - a hit amongst kids.

Youngsters prefer funky clothes (colourful T Shirts, faded denims) as compared to professionals who would go for subtle colours.

The target market of Zodiac Clothing Company Limited mainly comprises of office goers and professionals. The merchandise (shirts, trousers, neck ties, belts) is as per the taste of the professionals. Beach house shirts would have no takers in such a store.

- The merchandiser ideally works on the "invariant right" principle.

  Since most of us are right handed, it is a common tendency that customers entering into retail store would first go towards the right side of the store. The merchandiser should display the unique and expensive collections on the right side of the store to entice the customers.

- The set up of the store should be such that once a customer enters into a store, he has to walk through each and every department.
- The shelves should be stocked with the latest trends. The merchandise should be well organized on the racks according to their size and pattern.
- It is the key responsibility of the merchandiser to create an attractive display to pull the customers into the store. Once the customer steps into the store, he would definitely buy something or the other.

Visual Merchandising

The art of increasing the sale of products by effectively and sensibly displaying them at the retail outlet is called as visual merchandising. Visual merchandising refers to the aesthetic display of the merchandise to attract the potential buyers, prompt them to buy and eventually increase the sales of the store. In simpler words, visual merchandising is the art of displaying the merchandise to influence the consumer's buying behaviour.

The store must offer a positive ambience to the customers for them to enjoy their shopping.

The location of the products in the store has an important role in motivating the consumers to buy them. Sensible display of the merchandise goes a long way in influencing the buying decision of the individual.

The end-user will never notice something which is not well organized: instead stacked or thrown in heaps.

Proper Space, lighting, placing of dummies, colour of the walls, type of furniture,music, fragrance of the store all help in increasing the sale of the products.

Lighting is one of the critical aspects of visual merchandising. Lighting increases the visibility of the merchandise kept in the store. The store should be adequately lit and well ventilated. Avoid harsh lighting as it blinds the customers who walk into the store.

The signage displaying the name of the store or other necessary information must be installed properly outside the store at a place easily viewable to the customers even from a distance.

The retailer must be extremely cautious about the colour of the paint he chooses for his store. The paint colour can actually set the mood of the customers. The wall colours must be well coordinated with the carpet, floor tiles or the furnitures kept at the store. Dark colours make the room feel small and congested as compared to light and subtle colours.

The store must always smell good. Foul smell irritates the consumers and he would walk out of the store in no time. Use room fresheners 'or aromatic sticks for a pleasant environment.

The merchandise must be properly placed in display racks or shelves according to size and gender. Put necessary labels (size labels) on the shelves as it help the customers to locate the products easily. Make sure the product do not falls off the shelves as it gives a messy look.

The dummies should be intelligently placed and must highlight the unique collections, latest trends and new arrivals in order to catch the attention of the individual. The dummies should not act as an obstacle and should never be kept at the entrance of the store.

Don't play blaring music at the store. It acts as a hindrance to effective communication and the retailer can never understand what the buyer actually intends to buy.

Select the theme of the store according to the season. Red should be the dominating colour during Christmas or Valentines Day as the colour symbolizes love, fun and frolic. A white theme would look out of place during the season of love.

Don't keep unnecessary furniture as it gives a cluttered look to the store.

Why Visual Merchandising?

- Visual Merchandising helps the customers to easily find out what they are looking for.
- It helps the customers to know about the latest trends in fashion.
- The customer without any help can actually decide what he intends to buy.
- It increases the sales of the store and results in increased level of customer satisfaction.
- The customers can quickly decide what all they need and thus **visual merchandising makes shopping a pleasant experience**.
- Visual merchandising gives the store its unique image and makes it distinct from others.

Retail Management - Meaning and its Need

What is management ?

Management refers to the process of bringing people together on a common platform and make them work as a single unit to achieve the goals and objectives of an organization. Management is required in all aspects of life and forms an integral part of all businesses.

Retail management

The various processes which help the customers to procure the desired merchandise from the retail stores for their end use refer to retail management. Retail management includes all the steps required to bring the customers into the store and fulfill their buying needs.

Retail management makes shopping a pleasurable experience and ensures the customers leave the store with a smile. In simpler words, retail management helps customers shop without any difficulty.

Need for Retail Management - Why retail management ?

Peter wanted to gift his wife a nice watch on her birthday. He went to the nearby store to check out few options. The retailer took almost an hour to find the watches. This irritated Peter and he vowed not to visit the store again.-An example of poor management.

You just can't afford to make the customer wait for long. The merchandise needs to be well organized to avoid unnecessary searching. Such situations are common in mom and pop stores (kirana stores). One can never enjoy shopping at such stores.

Retail management saves time and ensures the customers easily locate their desired merchandise and return home satisfied.

An effective management avoids unnecessary chaos at the store.

Effective Management controls shopliftings to a large extent.

- The retailer must keep a record of all the products coming into the store.
- The products must be well arranged on the assigned shelves according to size, colour, gender, patterns etc.
- Plan the store layout well.
- The range of products available at the store must be divided into small groups comprising of similar products. Such groups are called categories. A customer can simply walk up to a particular category and look for products without much assistance.
- A unique SKU code must be assigned to each and every product for easy tracking.
- Necessary labels must be put on the shelves for the customers to locate the merchandise on their own.
- Don't keep the customers waiting.

- Make sure the sales representatives attend the customers well. Assist them in their shopping. Greet them with a smile
- The retailer must ensure enough stock is available at the store.
- Make sure the store is kept clean. Don't stock unnecessary furniture as it gives a cluttered look to the store. The customers must be able to move freely.
- The store manager, department managers, cashier and all other employees should be trained from time to time to extract the best out of them. They should be well aware of their roles and responsibilities and customer oriented. They should be experts in their respective areas.
- The store manager must make daily sales reports to keep a track of the cash flow. Use softwares or maintain registers for the same.
- Remove the unsold merchandise from the shelves. Keep them somewhere else.
- Create an attractive display.
- Plan things well in advance to avoid confusions later on.
- Ask the customers to produce bills in case of exchange. Assign fixed timings for the same. Don't entertain customers after a week.

Category Management

The mechanism of selling merchandise in small quantities from a fixed location directly to the individuals for their end use is called as retailing. The fixed location can be anything like super market, hyper market, department stores and so on.

Merchandise - Merchandise refers to the various products available at the store for sale to the end-users. It is the display of the merchandise which actually attracts the customers into the store.

Let us suppose all the products available at the store are stocked at one place only. Would such a display impress the customers ?

The answer is NO. Presentation of products is essential.

As a solution to the above problem, the retailers came out with the concept of category management.

The concept of segregating similar products into separate groups is called as category management. The complete range of merchandise available at the retail store is divided into separate product categories consisting of related products.

Categories in a retail store refer to the various groups which consist of products belonging to a similar family. The retailer smartly displays all the related products together as distinct categories for his as well as the end-user's convenience.

Example

Toothpaste, Tooth Brush, Mouth wash, Tongue cleaner, soap, shampoo, body wash, cosmetics etc, can be displayed together under a single category called personal care section.

Vegetables, Fruits, Tinned Food, Juice, meat, dairy products form a single category.

Certain retail stores also classify their merchandise into women, men as well as kids category.

Department stores also have separate categories like:

Apparels, Footwear, Jewellery, Electronic appliances, Mobiles, Watches, Home furnishings, house hold appliances and so on.

Category

- The complete range of merchandise at the store is divided into separate groups consisting of related products. Such groups are called as categories.
- Each category is treated as a separate business entity.
- The retailer calculates the profit and loss of each category separately.
- Each category contributes in its own way to the profitability of the store.
- The retailer does not promote a single brand but the complete category.
- The concept of categories has gone a long way in developing a strong bond between the retailer and the supplier.

Why Separate Categories ?

- The classification of products into separate category benefits the customers and makes their shopping a pleasurable experience.
- The customers as per their interest, pocket and need can walk up to the respective categories, check out the various options and decide what to buy and what not to buy.

Eight Step Process of category management

- Define the Category

The retailer must sort out the similar products which can be included in a single category. He must make sure that the products bear a strong connection with each other.

- Role of the Formed Category
- Evaluate the current Performance of the category
- Decide targets for the category.
- Devise an overall Strategy to promote the category.
- Formulate specific steps to increase the sales of the category.
- Implementation of the above steps.
- Review and feedback.

However some retailers find the above process cumbersome and only follow the below five steps:

- Form and Review the category.

- Decide the target consumers of the particular category.
- Planning and formulating strategies for the category.
- Implementation of the above strategies
- Results Evaluation

Category Captains

The retailer generally appoints one individual who supplies all the products of a single category. This individual also called as supplier is known as a category captain.

The suppliers are equally responsible for the category and contribute their level best to maximize the revenue of the particular category. He works in close coordination with the retailer and is responsible for the profit and loss of his assigned category.

Retail Marketing - Tips to Promote a Retail Brand

The mechanism of selling products in small quantities from fixed locations to the customers for their end use is called as retailing.

In the current scenario where the end-user has several options to rely on, it is essential that the retailer promotes his brand well amongst the masses.

Let us go through some **tips to promote a retail brand** well:

Signage

Signboards go a long way in creating brand awareness and promoting a particular brand.

- The signage must display the name as well as logo of the retail store.
- It must be installed at the right place visible to all even from a distance.
- It should not be very small. Small signages fail to attract the customers.
- Choose the right paint colour.
- Don't add unnecessary information. Keep it simple but informative.
- Make sure the signage attracts the customers into the store.
- Choose the right theme.

Advertising

Advertising is a strong medium which influences the buying decision of the customer and prompts him to shop. The retailer must ensure to communicate the USPs of his brand to the target customers well through various modes of advertising. The advertisement must be eye-catching for the end-users to click on them.

Various ways of Advertising

1. Billboards

Billboard is one of the best ways of out of home advertising.

Out of home advertising refers to creating awareness amongst the individuals when they are out of their homes.

- Install hoardings, banners, bill boards at strategic locations such as heavy traffic areas, major crossings, railway stations, bus stands etc to entice the customers. The retailer must ensure that the banners get noticed and bring results.
- Newspapers, Television and radio are also effective ways to promote a brand. Television reaches a wider audience and makes the store popular amongst all.
- The advertisement should be a visual treat, appeal the customers and prompt them to visit the store.

2. Coupons
- Coupons are an effective way of promoting a brand as they offer some kind of financial benefit to the customers in the form of discounts and rebates and thus attracting them into the store.
- Coupons help in furthering the brand image of the retail store without much investment.
- More and more people visit the stores to redeem the coupons, thus making the brand popular.
- Discounts, sale, rebates are good ways to promote a brand.

3. Private Label
- Private label is an effective way to promote one's brand at low costs.

- Products manufactured by one company but sold under another company's brand name are called Private Label Products.
- Create your own website.
- Print your own calendars, diaries, planners, table tops with your store's name, address as well as logo. Such an activity creates awareness among individuals.
- Always keep your visiting cards handy and distribute them to as many people as you can.
- In the current scenario, social networking sites go a long way in promoting brands. Create communities and invite people to join the same.
- Customer loyalty programs help to retain customers and attract new individuals to the store.
- Create a positive ambience at the store. Nothing works better than customer satisfaction in the retail industry. One satisfied customer brings ten new customers along with him.

Role of Advertising in Retail

Promoting a brand is more important than opening a store. It is essential to create brand awareness for the customers to know about the brand's existence. The retailer must strive hard to communicate the USPs (Unique selling Proposition) of the brand to influence the buying behaviour of the customers. In simpler words, advertisements help the end-users to know to which brand a particular product belongs.

Advertisements play a crucial role in promoting a brand and creating its awareness amongst the masses.

They help in creating an image of a particular product or brand in the minds of the potential customers. Such a mechanism is also called Brand Positioning.

What is Advertising ?

Advertising is a medium through which an individual or organization highlights the USPs and benefits of a product or service to influence the buying behaviour of the individuals.

It helps to create a positive image of a particular brand in the minds of the customers and prompts them to buy the same.

Role of Advertising in Retail

- The retailer through various ways of advertising strives hard to promote his brand amongst the masses for them to visit the store more often.
- Advertisements attract the customers into the store. They act as a catalyst in bringing the customers to the stores.

The advertisement must effectively communicate the right message and click on the customers. It should be a visual treat and appeal the end-users.

Advertisements have taglines to create awareness of a product or service in the most effective way.

- The tagline has to be crisp and impressive to create the desired impact.
- The tagline should not be lengthy else the effect gets nullified.
- It has to be catchy.
- It should be simple to memorize.

The moment an individual hears "Just Do it", he knows he has to visit a "Nike Store". That's the importance of a tagline.

Modes of Advertising

1. Nothing works better than promoting a brand through **signboards, billboards, hoardings and banners** intelligently placed at strategic locations like railway stations, crowded areas, heavy traffic crossings, bus stands, near cinema halls, residential areas and so on. Such advertising is also called as out of home advertising.

   Out of home advertising is a way to influence the individuals when they are out of their homes. The hoarding must be installed at a height visible to all even from a distance.

   Make sure it catches the attention of the passing individuals and influences them to visit the store.

Keep it simple and make sure it doesn't confuse the customers; instead it should convey the information in its desired form.

2. **Print media** is also one of the most effective ways to promote a brand. Newspapers, magazines, catalogues, journals make the brand popular amongst the individuals. Retailers can buy a small space in any of the leading newspapers or magazines; give their ads for the individuals to read and get influenced.

3. **Television** also helps the brand reach a wider audience. Now a days retailers also use celebrities to endorse their products for that extra zing. Celebrities are shown using the particular brand and thus making it a hit amongst the masses.

Sachin Tendulkar - the famous Indian cricketer endorses Castrol India, MRF tyres, Adidas, Boost etc.A child gets influenced to drink Boost because his favourite cricketer drinks the same.

4. **Radio Advertisements** also help in creating brand awareness.

5. **Social networking** sites have also emerged as one of the easiest and economical ways to promote a product or brand.

Retail Store Operations

Store Atmosphere

The store must offer a positive ambience to the customers for them to enjoy their shopping and leave with a smile.

- The store should not give a cluttered look.
- The products should be properly arranged on the shelves according to their sizes and patterns. Make sure products do not fall off the shelves.
- There should be no foul smell in the store as it irritates the customers.
- The floor, ceiling, carpet, walls and even the mannequins should not have unwanted spots.
- Never dump unnecessary packing boxes, hangers or clothes in the dressing room. Keep it clean.
- Make sure the customers are well attended.
- Don't allow customers to carry eatables inside the store.

Cash Handling

- One of the most important aspects of retailing is cash handling.
- It is essential for the retailer to track the daily cash flow to calculate the profit and loss of the store.
- Cash Registers, electronic cash management system or an elaborate computerized point of sale (POS) system help the retailer to manage the daily sales and the revenue generated.

Prevent Shoplifting/Safety and Security

- The merchandise should not be displayed at the entry or exit of the store.

- Do not allow customers to carry more than three dresses at one time to the trial room.
- Install CCTVs and cameras to keep a close watch on the customers.
- Each and every merchandise should have a security tag.
- Ask the individuals to submit carry bags at the security.
- Make sure the sales representative handle the products carefully.
- Clothes should not have unwanted stains or dust marks as they lose appeal and fail to impress the customers.
- Install a generator for power backup and to avoid unnecessary black outs.
- Keep expensive products in closed cabinets.
- Instruct the children not to touch fragile products.
- The customers should feel safe inside the store.

Customer Service

- Customers are assets of the retail business and the retailer can't afford to lose even a single customer.
- Greet customers with a smile.
- Assist them in their shopping.
- The sales representatives should help the individuals buy merchandise as per their need and pocket.
- The retailer must not oversell his products to the customers. Let them decide on their own.
- Give the individual an honest and correct feedback. If any particular outfit is not looking good on anyone, tell him the truth and suggest him some better options.

- Never compromise on quality of products. Remember one satisfied customer brings five more individuals to the store. Word of mouth plays an important role in Brand Promotion.

Refunds and Returns

- Formulate a concrete refund policy for your store.
- The store should have fixed timings for exchange of merchandise.
- Never exchange products in lieu of cash.
- Never be rude to the customer, instead help him to find something else.

Visual Merchandising

- The position of dummies should be changed frequently.
- There should be adequate light in the store. Change the burned out lights immediately.
- Don't stock unnecessary furniture at the store.
- Choose light and subtle colours for the walls to set the mood of the walk-ins.
- Make sure the signage displays all the necessary information about the store and is installed at the right place visible to all.
- The customers should be able to move and shop freely in the store.
- The retail store should be well ventilated.

Training Program

- The store manager must conduct frequent training programs for the sales representatives, cashier and other team members to motivate them from time to time.
- It is the store manager's responsibility to update his subordinates with the latest softwares in retail or any other developments in the industry.
- It is the store manager's responsibility to collate necessary reports (sales as well as inventory) and send to the head office on a daily basis.

Inventory and Stock Management

- The retailer must ensure to manage inventory to avoid being "out of stock".
- Every retail chain should have its own warehouse to stock the merchandise.
- Take adequate steps to prevent loss of inventory and stock.

Store Design and Layout - Different Floor Plans and Layouts

Opening a retail store is no joke and requires meticulous planning and detailed knowledge.

Location

Make sure your store is in a prime location and is easily accessible to the end-users. Do not open a store at a secluded place.

Floor Plan

The retailer must plan out each and everything well, the location of the shelves or racks to display the merchandise, the position of the mannequins or the cash counter and so on.

1. Straight Floor Plan

The straight floor plan makes optimum use of the walls, and utilizes the space in the most judicious manner. The straight floor plan creates spaces within the retail store for the customers to move and shop freely. It is one of the commonly implemented store designs.

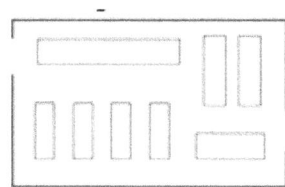

2. Diagonal Floor Plan

According to the diagonal floor plan, the shelves or racks are kept diagonal to each other for the owner or the store manager to have a watch on the customers. Diagonal floor plan works well in stores where customers have the liberty to walk in and pick up merchandise on their own.

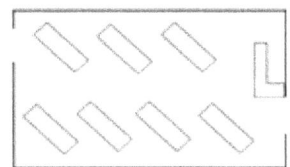

3. Angular Floor Plan

The fixtures and walls are given a curved look to add to the style of the store. Angular floor plan gives a more sophisticated look to the store. Such layouts are often seen in high end stores.

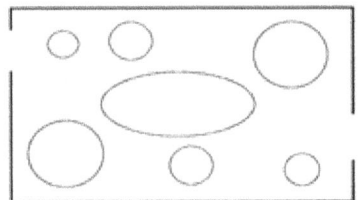

4. Geometric Floor Plan

The racks and fixtures are given a geometric shape in such a floor plan. The geometric floor plan gives a trendy and unique look to the store.

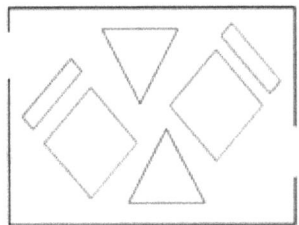

5. Mixed Floor Plan

The mixed floor plan takes into consideration angular, diagonal and straight layout to give rise to the most functional store lay out.

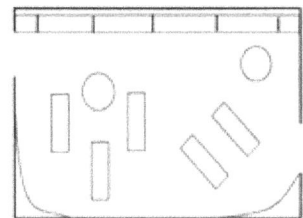

Tips for Store Design and Layout

- The signage displaying the name and logo of the store must be installed at a place where it is visible to all, even from a distance. Don't add too much information.
- The store must offer a positive ambience to the customers. The customers must leave the store with a smile.
- Make sure the mannequins are according to the target market and display the latest trends. The clothes should look fitted on the dummies without using unnecessary pins. The position of the dummies must be changed from time to time to avoid monotony.
- The trial rooms should have mirrors and must be kept clean. Do not dump unnecessary boxes or hangers in the dressing room.
- The retailer must choose the right colour for the walls to set the mood of the customers. Prefer light and subtle shades.
- The fixtures or furniture should not act as an object of obstacle. Don't unnecessary add too many types of furniture at your store.
- The merchandise should be well arranged and organized on the racks assigned for them. The shelves must carry

necessary labels for the customers to easily locate the products they need. Make sure the products do not fall off the shelves.

- Never play loud music at the store.
- The store should be adequately lit so that the products are easily visible to the customers. Replace burned out lights immediately.
- The floor tiles, ceilings, carpet and the racks should be kept clean and stain free.
- There should be no bad odour at the store as it irritates the customers.
- Do not stock anything at the entrance or exit of the store to block the way of the customers. The customers should be able to move freely in the store.
- The retailer must plan his store in a way which minimizes theft or shop lifting.
  - i. Merchandise should never be displayed at the entrance or exit of the store.
  - ii. Expensive products like watches, jewellery, precious stones, mobile handsets and so on must be kept in locked cabinets.
  - iii. Install cameras, CCTVs to have a closed look on the customers.
  - iv. Instruct the store manager or the sales representatives to try and assist all the customers who come for shopping.
  - v. Ask the customers to deposit their carry bags at the entrance itself.

vi.   Do not allow the customers to carry more than three dresses at one time to the trial room.

What is a Signage ?

Any visual representation which gives information to the customers about a store, any office, building, street, park and so on is called a signage.

Signage helps the customers to easily reach their desired destination or locate a building by simply following the instructions displayed on it.

Role of Signage in Retail Industry:

- A customer can easily locate the store with the help of a signage.
- **Signboard gives all necessary information about the store.** The customer can easily come to know about the products kept at the store without actually bothering anyone. Visual Displays put inside the retail store can actually help the customers to easily locate the merchandise.
- **It is the signboard which actually attracts the customers into the store.** The signage should be interesting enough to pull the customers into the store as a retailer can't afford to lose even a single customer.

- The signboard should not be too small. End-users might miss a small signage and hence the whole idea of attracting the customers into the store gets nullified.
- The signboards are an effective medium of communication between the retailer and the customer.
- The signboard gives the store its unique identity and helps in furthering its brand image.
- A signage goes a long way in influencing the customer's buying decision. A single glance at the signboard helps the customer to decide whether he has to step into the store or not?

Important points to keep in mind while installing Signage

- The signage should never block the entrance of the store. It should not hide the interiors of the store.
- Install the signage at a place which can be easily viewed by all even from a distance.
- The signboard must display all the necessary information like the name of the store, its logo or any other required information.
- Don't put too much information on the signboard. Let the customers walk into the store and find out on their own what the store is offering.
- A single word "Discount" written on the signboard outside the store can do the trick. The customer would be inquisitive enough to find out what the store offers. He would definitely step into the store to check out the various options. There is actually no need to mention how much discount, what percentage and so on.

- The material and the fabric used for the signboard should be of premium quality so that it lasts for a longer duration. The retailer must make sure the signboard does not lose its lustre.
- Choose the right paint for the signage. Make sure the information is clearly visible to all. The customers should be able to easily read the signboard even from a distance. Choose a light background colour and a dark text colour for clear visibility. One can also highlight the important information. Don't pick any colour which might make your signboard look dull.
- The name of the store should be written in bold or in a different font to create the desired impact.
- Design your signboard in the most unique and innovative way for the customers to get attracted into the store.
- The signboard should not mislead or confuse the customers.
- Keep the signboard simple but informative.

Role of Coupons in Retail Marketing

What is Retailing ?

The sale of products to the customers from a fixed location (malls, department stores, super markets and so on) in small quantities for their end use is called as retailing.

Coupons play an important role in promoting the retail stores and making the brand popular amongst the masses.

What are Coupons ?

Any document which can be presented to the retailer to gain some kind of financial benefit in the form of discount on any product is called a coupon. Customers can get the coupons redeemed at the specific retail outlets to avail relevant discounts and rebates in shopping.

Role of Coupons in Retail Marketing

- Coupons play an important role in attracting the customers into the store.
- Coupons help in furthering the brand image of the retail store without huge investments. It makes the brand popular among the end-users. Individuals talk more about the brand, thus making it a hit amongst the masses.

What is Guerrilla Marketing ?

The concept of promoting products and brands on an extremely low budget is called as Guerrilla Marketing. Guerrilla marketing does not involve huge investments and is one of the most effective ways of creating brand awareness amongst the consumers.

Coupons are an effective tool for Guerrilla Marketing. The retailers can actually create brand awareness amongst the end users without spending much with the help of coupons.

How does Coupons help in Guerrilla Marketing ?

- A Coupon is one of the most cost effective ways of promoting the brand with little investment.
- Coupons make the brand popular as more and more customers visit the store to redeem their coupons.

Example - As a part of their marketing strategy, on every purchase of Domino's pizza, the company offers discount coupons to the buyers. These discount coupons can be availed next time the customer places his order.

In such a situation, it is more likely that he would visit a Domino's Outlet again to redeem his coupons and avail the discounts on the pizza. He would generally not prefer any other outlet as here in Domino's he can get pizza at a lesser price as compared to others.

Dominos in this case used food coupons to attract the customers once again into the store.

- Coupons go a long way in influencing the buying behaviour of the customers.
- Coupons also bring in new customers to the store. The individuals, who do not even know about a particular brand, visit the store to use their coupons and also check out other options as well.
- Coupons also benefit the customers as they can now purchase their desired merchandise at a lower cost.
- Coupons increase the store traffic and also result in Impulse Buying.

What is Impulse Buying ?

Any unplanned buying is called as Impulse Buying. An individual might not require a particular product but picks it up out of mere emotions and feelings. Such a buying is called impulse buying. Impulse buying prompts the customer to purchase products which he might not even need that time.

Peter went to a retail store to redeem his discount coupons on shirts. The retailer had smartly displayed perfumes near the cash counter. While paying the bill, Peter could not resist purchasing two perfumes for himself along with the shirts. An example of Impulse Buying.

Factors Affecting Buying Decision of the Customers at the Store

There are several factors which affect the buying decision of the customers. Let us go through them one by one:

1. **Store Display and Presentation of Products**

   The **store display plays an important role in influencing the buying decision of the customers**. It is the display of the store which attracts passing individuals into the store. The store must have an attractive display to entice the customers. Shopping may be the last priority for an individual but a creative display encourages him to spend on shopping.

- A retailer must intelligently display the latest trends on mannequins to prompt the customers to buy the same.
- Make sure the products are kept on their respective racks. The merchandise should not fall off the shelves.
- Since most of us are right handed; we tend to go towards the right side of the store, the moment we step inside. The retailer must thus display expensive and unique merchandise on the right side of the store.
- Remove old stock from the shelves.

2. Ambience of the Store

The **store ambience plays an important role in attracting new customers and retaining existing ones**.

- A customer would never purchase anything from a store which is not clean. Foul smell irritates individuals and thus they leave in no time.
- Play soulful music for a positive effect on the customers.
- The store should be well lit and ventilated for the customers to enjoy their shopping.

3. Customer Treatment

Warm customer treatment is an effective way to pull the customers into the store. It is essential for the retailers to treat the customers like kings to expect loyalty from them.

- Understand your customers well. Try to find out what they expect from the store.
- The sales representative must greet the customers with a warm smile. It makes a difference.
- Assist them in their shopping.
- Never oversell.
- The retailer must never lie to the customers. If something is not looking good on them, be honest and give them a correct feedback.
- If a customer comes for an exchange, don't be rude; instead help him with an alternative.

4. Store Design and Layout

A customer would never prefer shopping from a store which gives a cluttered look.

- There should be ample space in the store for the customers to move and shop freely.
- Put stickers and labels (size, colour, FS (Full sleeves), HS (Half Sleeves) and so on) on the shelves and racks.
- Don't stock unnecessary furniture and fixtures in the store.
- Classify the complete range of merchandise into small groups (categories) comprising of similar and related products. Categories help the customers to locate the products easily.
- A store must have a trial (change) room.

- Individuals avoid places where there is a parking hassle. The store should have an adequate parking space.

5. **Other Factors**
- Discounts and rebates influence the customers to shop more. A customer might not need a product, but a discount will encourage him to purchase the same as he would now get it at a lower price.
- Promotional schemes like free gifts also affect the buying decision of the customers. A Free T Shirt with a pair of jeans would definitely prompt the customers to shop more.
- Customers also indulge in shopping to redeem their coupons and avail discounts.

Tips to be a Successful Retailer

- Opening a retail store is no joke. It demands dedication, detailed study and meticulous planning. An individual must do his groundwork well. **Plan things well in advance to avoid problems later on**.
- It is important to do some kind of research work before taking the big leap. **Browse through related websites to gain an in-depth knowledge**.
- **An individual must be well aware of the fundamentals of retail industry to have an edge over others**. Short term courses in retail make an individual well versed with the basic concepts of retailing, store

formats, visual merchandising and so on which eventually help him in the long run.

- **Know what is happening around you**. Keep yourself updated with the latest trends in the retail industry. Check out various fashion magazines, brochures, catalogues, newspapers for the latest developments.
- **Know your target market well**. Find out more about the tastes and preferences to meet their expectations.
- It is important to **choose the right location for the store** to ensure maximum walk-ins. Make sure the store is well connected by means of transportation. Don't open store at a secluded place.
- Make sure there is **adequate parking space** near your store.
- **Promote your store well**. It is essential to create awareness of your brand amongst the customers for them to know about the brand's existence. Devise strategies to make your brand popular amongst the masses.
- Create the company's website and get your visiting cards printed.
- **Set a budget for everything**.
- The products stocked in the store and their display play an important role in attracting the customers into the store. **A retailer must never compromise on quality of the merchandise**. Visit various wholesalers to check out the latest trends. Pick up something which is unique and not available at any other store. Don't stock things

which are out of fashion. The merchandise should be as per the target market and location of the store.

- Visit few other retail outlets to get an idea about store designs and layouts.
- Hire trained employees for your store. The employees must be well aware of their roles and responsibilities for them to deliver their best. Motivate them from time to time through various training programmes, appraisals, incentives and other monetary benefits.
- Be patient and don't rush into things.
- **Plan your store layout well**. Make sure there is ample space inside the store for the customers to move and shop freely.
- Don't dump products. Use shelves, cabinets and almirahs to stock your merchandise.
- **Be disciplined**. Open your store on time and assign fixed timings for lunch and tea.
- **Treat your customers as kings**. Advise all the store members to be courteous with the customers. The sales representatives must assist the customers in their shopping and make sure they leave the store with a smile.
- **Never oversell**. Let the customers decide on their own what would look good on them.
- **Manage your inventory well**.
- It is important for the retailer to track the cash flow.
- Download various retail softwares to make your work easier and effective.

Roles and Responsibilities of a Store Manager

Retail Store

A fixed set up or location offering merchandise in small quantities to the consumers for their end-use is called a retail store.

Store Manager

- An individual responsible for managing the overall functioning of the store is called a store manager.
- A store manager takes care of the day to day operations of the store and ensures maximum profitability for his store.

In simpler words a retail store is a store manager's baby.

Hierarchy

General   Manager
↑
Store   Manager
↑
**All   employees   of   the   store
(Floor manager, cashier, Department manager, Asst Store manager)**

Gender Preference

Both Male/Female. However in certain cases the selection might depend on the merchandise available in the store. A store specializing in female lingerie would prefer a female store manager as she would be more comfortable with the female buyers.

Responsibilities of the Store Manager

- **Recruiting employees for the store is the store manager's prime responsibility**. He not only has to hire the right candidates for the store but also train them for their overall development. He must ensure that all the employees (floor manager, department manager, cashier and so on) contribute to their level best for the effective functioning of the store. He must act as a strong pillar of support and stand by his team at the hour of crisis. It is his duty to acquaint his team members with the latest trends in fashion or any other newly launched retail software. It is his responsibility to delegate responsibilities to his subordinates according to their specializations and extract the best out of them. The store manager must motivate his team members from time to time.

- **The store manager must make sure his store is meeting the targets and earning profits**. He is responsible for the smooth and effective functioning of the store.

- **The store manager is responsible for maintaining the overall image of the store**. It is his duty to sensibly display the merchandise so that it immediately catches the attention of the customers. The store manager must ensure that his store meets the expectations of the customers and lives up to its predefined brand image.

He must ensure:

i.   The store is kept clean
ii. Shelves and racks are properly stocked and products do not fall off the shelves.
iii. Mannequins are kept at the right place to attract the customers into the store and rotated frequently.
iv. The merchandise should be according to the season as well as the latest trends.
v.   The store is well lit, ventilated and offers a positive ambience to the customers.
vi. The signage displaying the name and logo of the store is installed at the right place and viewable to all.

- One of the major responsibilities of the store manager is to make the customers feel safe and comfortable in the store. It is his key responsibility to make sure that the customer leaves the store with a pleasant smile.

- **He is responsible for managing the assets of the store**. The security and safety of the store is his responsibility. The store manager must ensure that sufficient inventory is available at the store to avoid being "out of stock".

- He along with his subordinates are responsible for planning, managing profit and loss, handling cash at the store as well as collating daily sales as well as other necessary reports.

- He must ensure that the store is free from pilferage.

What are Mannequins ? - Purpose and its Importance in Retail Industry

Visual Merchandising plays an important role in increasing the sales of any retail store. The presentation and display of the merchandise play an important role in attracting the customers into the store and prompting them to buy the products.

Mannequins in simpler words also called as dummies play an important role in visual merchandising.

What are Mannequins ?

The artificial dolls used by the retailers to display their merchandise (can be anything) are called as mannequins. The mannequins help the customers to know about the latest trend the store offers without sometimes even bothering the sales representative. It is the attractive mannequin which pulls the customer into the store.

Purpose of Mannequins

- Mannequins are used to highlight the unique collections of the store.

- Mannequins display the latest trends in fashion and influence the customers to buy the particular merchandise.
- Mannequins attract the customers into the store and thus increase the revenue and profit.
- Mannequins are also responsible for up selling at the retail store.

What is Up Selling ?

Up selling is a sales mechanism where the sales representative strives hard to convince the customers to buy extra items or expensive merchandise and thus increases the revenue of the store. The entire credit goes to the sales representative in case of up selling who influences the customers to take home additional and expensive merchandise in addition to what they are already buying.

Example

- A customer goes to a retail store to buy a watch worth x rupees. The sales representative through his unique presentation skills convinces the customer to buy another model worth y rupees where y > x.
- A customer might go to purchase a single pair of footwear. It is upselling when the sales man influences the customer to buy two pairs instead of one.

How do Mannequins help in upselling ?

Mannequins help the customers to understand what would look good on them. The customer might not understand how a particular bag would look with a particular dress or for that matter which fashion jewellery would add elegance to a particular outfit.

The retailer must smartly decide the entire look of the mannequin.

Sandra went to buy a nice dress for her office party. The mannequin wearing a blue dress at a retail store immediately caught her attention and she decided to buy it. The retailer had sensibly also added a blue neckpiece and a trendy clutch to the mannequin for the complete look.

Sandra was not very sure what she wanted to wear along with the dress. The moment she saw the mannequin she knew what would look good on her. Not only did she purchase the dress but also the neckpiece along with the clutch. An example of upselling.Sometimes you can't decide what all would look good on you; a mannequin helps you decide the same.

Points to be considered while choosing a Mannequin

- Make sure the mannequin is not too heavy.
- The shape and size of the mannequin must be according to your target market.
- The mannequins must not act as an object of obstacle.
- It should never be kept at the entrance or the exit door as it blocks the way of the potential buyers.

- The clothes should look properly fitted on the mannequin. Avoid using unnecessary pins.
- Carefully select what you want your mannequin to wear.
- Change the position of the mannequins frequently.
- The mannequins should not be dirty or have unwanted stains.
- The clothes on the mannequins should be according to the season and changed at regular intervals to avoid monotony.

Types of Mannequins

- Abstract Mannequins
- Headless Mannequins
- Realistic Mannequins
- Tailors Dummies
- Display Forms

Planograms - Meaning, its Need and Types of Product Placements

How do you think buildings are constructed ?

With the help of architectural drawings.

An architectural drawing creates a rough print of the building on paper which gives an idea about the floor plans, location of rooms, lobby and so on.

In retail a planogram replaces architectural drawings.

Once a retailer opens a store, he needs to have a rough idea about the store plan. A planogram helps in the same.

Planograms are similar to architectural drawings and help the retailer to understand where the merchandise should be stocked in order to catch the customer's attention and make the maximum impact.

Planograms are nothing but diagrams which give the retailer an idea how and where to place the merchandise to attract the customers into the store.

Need for Planograms - Why Planograms ?

Presentation of product plays an important role at the retail store. With the help of Planograms; a retailer can actually know where to place the products for the maximum effect.

Planogram enables the retailers to stock the products at the right place and at the right time to attract the customers and prompt them to buy.

A retailer can make the best possible use of the available space with the help of planograms.

The merchandiser can actually create an attractive display to entice the customers with the help of planograms.

Planograms indirectly also contribute in maximizing the sale of the merchandise and thus generate revenues for the store. A cluttered store fails to attract the customers. The planograms help the retailer to arrange the products in the best possible way for the customers to pick up almost everything.

When is a Planogram Prepared ?

A Planogram ideally should be prepared before the merchandise reaches the retail store. The retailer should be very clear where he wants to place his products to impress the customers.

How is a Planogram Prepared ?

There are various softwares available which help to create planograms. These softwares help the retailers to draw three dimensional diagrams of the store and help them visualize the overall image of the store.

Types of Merchandise Placement

Visual Product Placement - Visual Product Placement refers to a technique where the products are placed in a way to immediately catch the attention of the customers walking into the store.

Types of Visual Product Placement

1. Horizontal Product Placement

According to horizontal product placement, products are placed side by side on shelves to offer a wide range of options to the customers.

2. Vertical product placement

The vertical product placement displays the merchandise on more than one shelf level.

3. Block Placement

According to block placement of products, the related products or merchandise belonging to a similar family are stocked at one place together under one common umbrella.

4. Commercial Product Placement

Commercial product placement takes into account the brand value of the merchandise. Every customer has a perceived image of the merchandise which decides its placement in the store. A product which has several takers would definitely get the best position as compared to something which does not contribute much to the revenue of the store.

5. Market share product placement

Market share product placement plan works on a simple strategy:

A product which generates the maximum revenue for the store should ideally be placed at a prime location for the customers to notice it and immediately buy it.

6. Margin Product Placement

According to Margin product placement, the more a product earns profit for the retailer, the better the location it is placed.

Inventory Management in Retail Industry - Need and Important Terminologies

What is Inventory Management ?

Inventory refers to the goods stocked for future use. Every retail chain has its own warehouse to stock the merchandise to be used when the existing stock replenishes.

Inventory management refers to the storage of products to be used at the time of crisis.

The retailer keeps a track of the stocked goods and makes sure there is surplus inventory to avoid being "out of stock". Such a process is called as inventory management.

Why Inventory Management ?

Gone are the days when customers had limited options for shopping. In the current scenario, if a customer does not find the desired merchandise at one retail shop, he has a second brand to rely on. A retailer can't afford to loose even a single customer. It is really important for the retailer to retain his existing customers as well as attract potential buyers. The retailer must ensure that every customer leaves his store with a smile. Unavailability of merchandise, empty shelves leave a negative impression on the customers and they are reluctant to visit the store in near future. Inventory management prevents such a situation.

One must understand that the products need some time to reach the store from the supplier's unit. The retailer must have sufficient stock to offer to the customers during the "lead time".

Managing inventory also helps the retailer during situations beyond control like transport strikes, curfews etc. The retailer has ample stock as a result of judicious inventory management even at the time of crisis.

Important Terminologies used in Inventory management

1. SKU (Stock Keeping Unit)

Every product available at the store has a unique code. This code which helps in the identification and tracking of the products at the retail store is called as stock keeping unit or SKU.

The retailer feeds each and every SKU in the master computer and can easily track the product in the stock just by entering the SKU Number.

Assigning a unique code to the products avoids unnecessary searching.

Example

Let us take the example of "Numero Uno" which stocks denims, shirts, T Shirts and targets both men as well as women.

SKU for Shirts

- NU – M–40-FL-W
- NU - M-38-FL-B

Where:

NU	stands	for	Numero	Uno
M		-		Men
40		-	Collar	Size
FL		-	Full	Sleeves

W - White (Colour of the shirt)

In the same way B in the second example would stand for Blue

Simply typing NU – M–40-FL-W would let the retailer know whether the particular merchandise is available with him or not.

2. New Old Stock (Abbreviated as NOS)

The stock which is never been sold by the retailer and now not even being manufactured comprises the new old stock. Such products do not have takers and may not be produced anymore.

3. Stock out

Stock out refers to a situation when the retailer fails to fulfill the customer's requirement due to lack of merchandise. The merchandise is not available in the current inventory and thus the customer has to return home empty handed.

Preventing loss of inventory

Employees working at the store might get tempted to steal the merchandise.

Let us go through some tips which help to prevent loss of inventory:

- Check the bags of the employees before they leave the store.
- Raise an alarm whenever you find someone stealing something. Supporting a wrong deed is also a crime.
- Make sure that all the employees leave from one common door.
- Avoid multiple exits.
- Check garbage before dumping.
- Keep proper record of the inventory(Stock coming in and going out)

www.ingramcontent.com/pod-product-compliance
Lightning Source LLC
Chambersburg PA
CBHW080830180526
45168CB00006B/2635